A Study Of The Lord's Prayer

William R. Richards

A STUDY OF
THE LORD'S PRAYER

A Study

OF

The Lord's Prayer

BY

WILLIAM R. RICHARDS

PASTOR OF THE BRICK PRESBYTERIAN CHURCH
NEW YORK CITY

PHILADELPHIA

The Westminster Press

MCMIX

1337

FOREWORD

THE aim of the following study is to call attention to certain features of our Lord's teaching as exhibited in the prayer which bears his name. On such a theme one may hardly hope to say anything that has not often been said before, but some things are worth saying over and over.

Especially the prayer always reminds us that the human brotherhood into which Jesus urged his disciples rests on a faith in the divine fatherhood; and that if we want a righteous democracy among men we must pray for the kingdom of God.

W. R. R.

THE BRICK CHURCH, New York.

September, 1909.

CONTENTS

The Lord's Prayer

Our Father which art in heaven, Hallowed be thy name. Thy kingdom come. Thy will be done in earth, as it is in heaven. Give us this day our daily bread. And forgive us our debts, as we forgive our debtors. And lead us not into temptation, but deliver us from evil: For thine is the kingdom, and the power, and the glory, for ever. Amen.

THE LORD'S PRAYER

INTRODUCTION

Teach Us to Pray

"Lord, teach us to pray," said one of the disciples; but was not the Lord always doing this for them? What was his own living example but one long, uninterrupted course of instruction in the duty and privilege of prayer to God?

Those who came nearest to Jesus evidently felt that he was one who lived consciously and constantly in a divine presence. John the Baptist down by the Jordan bank seemed to see the divine Spirit, in bodily form like a dove, descending and abiding upon him. Martha said, "I know that whatsoever thou wilt ask of God, God will give it thee," intimating the same sense of continual communion. Jesus himself used to

9

speak to his disciples about his Father as
one without whom not even a sparrow could
fall to the ground; one, therefore, who
could be trusted to take good care of them;
one who knew all their needs and could be
trusted at all times and everywhere to keep
them safe. To use a phrase that has grown
dear to some of us in these later times, Jesus
was one who had made a "practice of the
presence of God." And the disciples knew
this, felt it. What the old patriarch had
once seen in his dream at night they seemed
to behold in the waking hours of every day:
"the heaven open, and the angels of God
ascending and descending upon the Son
of man." But what was all this but teaching them the very deepest part of the lesson of prayer? For if you have learned
to feel God, and to trust him as one always
near you, always looking upon you, always
listening to you, always caring for you, the
rest of the lesson could not be very difficult. It is the most natural thing in the

world to speak to your friend—when you have anything to say to him—if only you know that you have a friend and that he is here.

But though Christ's whole life was thus a life of constant prayerfulness or communion, he also offered his disciples the example of setting apart particular times for praying. And I think there is no other part of our Lord's example that most of us need to be more careful in copying than this. For it has come to be the fashion with some excellent people not to think much of special times for prayer, but to insist more upon the duty of active service for men. To make sure of getting your day's work done; to spend your days going about doing good; to use your time to feed the hungry and clothe the naked and heal the sick—that will be to spend your life as Jesus Christ did, so men say—that will be far better than burying yourself uselessly in some quiet convent for undisturbed prayer to God. "To labor is to pray," they say; "he prayeth best who loveth best." And all that is very true, and a most important Christian truth in its proper place. But if we are really trying to learn these truths from the example of Jesus, then we must not forget to ask also where it was that he himself sought and found the strength that should make possible all those days of extraordinary activity and usefulness. And it is not difficult to learn where he found it if one really wishes to know.

In one place in the record you will read how he healed a demoniac child whom his disciples had been laboring over in vain. And when they asked him afterwards why their own efforts had been so fruitless, when his were so successful, he answered, "This kind goeth not out but by prayer." And if you read back you will learn that he himself had, in fact, just come down from the Mountain of Transfiguration, and that he had gone up into that mount to pray. Now if any of us are trying to imitate Christ's life of active usefulness on the plain without following also the other part of his example when he went up into the mount to pray, it is likely that many of our efforts will be as fruitless as were those of these puzzled disciples.

And this was not an isolated or peculiar incident. The narrative makes it clear that Jesus very often went away thus alone by himself, or with only two or three companions, to pray. It is true he was in some sense praying all the while and everywhere; that is, in the sense that he lived constantly in the assurance of his Father's presence with him. But that was not enough for Christ. He must have times when he could pray and give his whole mind to it. It seems to have been his custom before any great emergency to seek out such opportunity for undisturbed prayer to his Father.

Before he picked out the twelve men who
were to be called apostles and to work
with him and after him in founding his
church, we read that "he went out into a
mountain to pray, and continued all night
in prayer to God." "When it was day," it
says, he came down among the people and
resumed his active work among them.

And so afterwards, when the last great
emergency of his life was close at hand
and when he was about to be given into the
power of his enemies, he sought the shaded
solitude of the Garden of Gethsemane that
he might pray. That one last night of his
life may be taken as a very important part
of the instruction that Jesus offered his
disciples on this subject. "Lord, teach us
to pray," was their request, and here in
the garden he was teaching them.

How many different bits of teaching he
gave them on this subject during the hours
of that one night. First, when he took the
bread and the cup and blessed them—for

evidently this had been his custom whenever he and others were eating together.
Whether he was feeding the five thousand
on the hillside in Galilee, or his twelve
friends in the upper chamber in Jerusalem,
or just two of them in the stopping place at
Emmaus, his custom was, as he took the
bread, to speak his thanks to God before
he ate it. This gesture of courtesy toward
the divine Benefactor was so habitual with
him that it was the first thing those two disciples at Emmaus knew him by after he was
risen from the grave. The Master "was
known of them in breaking of bread."
When we ask that "the grace of the Lord
Jesus Christ" may be with us all, it is well
to remember that one characteristic exhibi-
tion of this gracious quality in him was the
habit of saying grace before meat.

Then, for a second word of instruction,
Christ warned his overconfident disciple
Peter that a sifting of temptation was
about to fall upon them all: "But I have

prayed for thee," he said to Peter, "that thy faith fail not." Those who wish the Lord to teach them to pray as he prayed must study that part of his example when he prayed for his friends. By all means manifest your friendliness by friendly deeds, feeding your friends when hungry, clothing and sheltering them when they are cold, and healing them when they are sick, for Christ's example encourages us to such helpful activities; but you are not following his example through unless you also pray for your friends.

Then follows that prayer related in the seventeenth chapter of John, when these eleven friends of Jesus heard him praying for them all, and for all who should believe through their word.

And then last of all comes the prayer in the Garden, when the storm broke over our Lord's own soul, and the bewildered disciples heard their Master praying for himself: "O my Father, if it be possible, let this cup pass from me: nevertheless, not as I will, but as thou wilt." And then again the second time they heard him say, "O my Father, if this cup may not pass away from me, except I drink it, thy will be done."

On this night some of the disciples were near enough to overhear how he prayed for himself. We have no report of what he had said on other of those long nights of watching when he had been alone with God. We do not know how often on earlier occasions he may have felt something of the bitterness of the cup appointed him to drink, offering up his prayer and supplication with strong crying and tears. Only once, on this last night of the long life struggle, there were witnesses near enough to overhear, and to tell us afterwards how Jesus used to pray for himself.

So that one night, the last night of our Lord's earthly life, gives us from his example this fourfold instruction on the subject of prayer: first, when he thanked God for his good gift of bread; then, when he prayed for his friend Peter; then, when he prayed for all his friends and for others; then, when he prayed for himself. When any disciple says, "Lord, teach us to pray," he must be ready to take his teaching—the best kind of teaching—from the example of the Master when he prayed. No other part of our Lord's example demands a more careful study from his disciples. It is not reasonable to suppose that any disciple can follow Christ successfully in the kind of active work that he was always doing for men who has not also learned from him something of the secret of his strength for doing that work.

What does any great city most need from the churches in it in order that the people may be helped as they would be helped if Jesus in bodily form were walking about the streets? Some may answer that the chief need is of a more generous supply of coats and hats and shoes, or more spacious orphanages and hospitals. But whenever the need of such purchasable commodities is made sufficiently evident, you hardly know what to do with the abundance of the contributions offered.

What is needed most, and this need is not so quickly supplied, is that, of those called Christians, there should be more who have learned from the Master to make a practice of the presence of God; so that whenever we speak of him it shall be in the tone of men who know; and when a hard bit of work has to be done we can do it with the kind of strength that came to the Master from prayer; and when some dark trouble or fierce temptation falls, staggering men's faith, we can meet it as he met his after he had watched and prayed in Gethsemane.

That appalling disaster of a few months ago in southern Italy, which plunged a nation into mourning and stirred the sympathy of the world, made large claim for material help, and the help was promptly offered; but was there not, and is there not, still greater need throughout that stricken and desolate region of men and women who could face even such dreadful trouble and still cling to their trust in a God who loves? Where can you learn such faith except from him who could look forward upon the black mystery of the cross itself, while his soul was in agony and his sweat as it were great drops of blood falling to the ground, and still say, "Father, if this cup may not pass away from me, except I drink it, thy will be done."

Yes, the greatest blessing that the churches could confer would be a supply of disciples who had learned from their Master's example how to pray.

The following chapters attempt a brief study of the sentences of the Lord's Prayer, but the best introduction to any such study is to recall first the personal example of the Lord himself and how he prayed.

CHAPTER I

Our Father

We have seen in the introductory chapter that our Lord by his own example was always teaching his disciples to pray; but when a specific request for such instruction came from one of the disciples, what the man himself intended to ask for was some form of words that might properly be used in their supplications. Such a form was furnished them, and from that day to this the disciples have loved to use it in their prayers to God. And we never tire of studying it as a model for all our praying, even when we might not word our requests according to this particular form.

The successive chapters of this little book are studies of the successive petitions of this form of prayer which Christ taught to his disciples.

"But when ye pray," he said, and as good old Matthew Henry says, "it is taken for granted that all the disciples of Christ pray. As soon as ever Paul was converted, 'behold, he prayeth.' You may as soon find a living man that doth not breathe as a Christian that doth not pray." "When ye pray, . . . after this manner therefore pray ye."

"Our Father," and that one opening phrase of the prayer will furnish material enough for this first chapter.

May I quote here another quaint observation from old Matthew Henry: "The Lord's Prayer (as indeed every prayer) is a letter sent from earth to heaven. Here is the inscription of the letter, the person to whom it is directed, 'Our Father'; the place, where, 'in heaven'; the contents of it, in several errands of request; the close, 'for thine is the kingdom'; the seal, 'Amen'; and if you will, the date, too, 'this day.'"

This chapter will be taken up with the inscription—the person to whom this letter is addressed, "Our Father."

The question has been much discussed by students of the Bible how far the several phrases of this prayer were original with Christ; or whether he may have selected them from phrases already familiar to the Jews in their customs of worship. Some of them must have been familiar, for some evident parallels have been pointed out; but Canon Plumptre seems justified in saying that "these parallels do not carry us very far." At all events, however it be with the separate phrases, this Lord's Prayer as a whole was altogether original with Christ in the new spirit which breathes through and unifies all its sentences. Preeminently is that true of this opening phrase, this name for the God to whom the prayer is to be offered.

The ancient Hebrews, like our own Indians and other primitive peoples, made much of names. The names they claimed for themselves or gave to their children were always understood to mean something, something indicative of the character or circumstances of the person named. And so it must be with the name for God—it was far more than a sound; it was the disclosure of God himself. To the mind of a devout Hebrew there could be no more vitally interesting religious question than, What is God's real name?

We read of Jacob in that crowning spiritual experience that we call his wrestling, that he said to the mysterious Antagonist, "Tell me thy name." The name was not told then. But we read afterwards of Moses, in the hour of his great experience by the burning bush, that he asked a similar question of the Presence that had been ordering him to Egypt; by what name should Moses speak of God to the people in Egypt; and the name was told, "I am." "I am hath sent thee." The early patriarchs had known God only as the Almighty; now it is the "I am," Jehovah. First came the thought of God as power; now the deeper thought of God as being.

But Christ does not put either of those names at the head of his prayer; it is "Father," and our question is how far this title is original with Christ, how generally this word "Father" had come into Jewish usage as a true name for God in prayer.

Of course, you can find some hints at such a usage—not very many—in the books of our Old Testament. As where, in Deuteronomy [1] or Isaiah [2] or Malachi,[3] the people are rebuked as disobedient and disrespectful children. Malachi says, speaking for God, "If then I be a father, where is my honor?" Or again God is sometimes appealed to as the last resource of those who have no other, as in Isaiah [4] one is heard crying, "Doubtless thou art our

[1] Ch. 32 : 6. [2] Ch. 1 : 2. [3] Ch. 1 : 6. [4] Ch. 63 : 16.

father, though Abraham be ignorant of us, and Israel acknowledge us not." Or again the psalmist cries,[5] "When my father and my mother forsake me, then the Lord will take me up." But the passages are not many. No such name would stand in their common forms of prayer.

In those later Hebrew writings which we call the Apocrypha, these hints at a faith in the fatherhood of God become somewhat more common; as where the son of Sirach [6] calls God the Father and Governor of all his whole life, or where Tobit declares that "God is our Father for ever." It is evident that the sound of this name at least would not be altogether unfamiliar to our Lord's Jewish hearers. And, indeed, heathen as well as Jews had sometimes spoken of the divine being as a sort of parent to the creation: "Zeus the father of gods and men." But that this name

[5] Ps. 27 : 10. [6] Ch. 23 : 1.

should be used as Jesus was now encouraging them to use it, used by every disciple at the beginning of every prayer—this was a religious phenomenon without precedent. That any one plain man in his own daily personal prayer should venture to say, ''Father,'' as if that were name enough; as if that told all that we ever need to tell about the God whom we wish our prayer to reach;—there never was a more original contribution to human thought than when Jesus spoke this opening phrase in the prayer which he was teaching for all his disciples, and so for the whole world.

But here let me recur for a moment to what was said in the introductory chapter, that our Lord did more than furnish a form of words for prayer, that his own example had been for these men one long course of instruction in the subject of prayer. Indeed if it had not been so, if this new name for God had been a form of words and nothing else, it is quite certain that the world would never have learned it so as to remember and use it. But it was very much more than a form; it came from a speaker who himself always began his prayers in this way. It was by his own example that Jesus was teaching men, and has taught men whenever they pray to say, "Father."

There are two peculiarities to be noticed in the religious situation of our time; the one is that to many it seems increasingly difficult to believe that the unseen power which made and rules the world can be like a father; but the other peculiar fact of the times is that if we are to go on praying at all we must now believe in the fatherhood of him to whom we pray.

That first difficulty of believing that God is like a father arises from our wider observation of the stern facts of the universe. The apparent heartlessness of it weighs upon our souls like an intolerable burden. The very phrases that our later teachers have taught us: "natural selection," "the struggle for existence," "the survival of the fittest"—what a hopeless, Godless sound they have! Or again, when the earthquake swallowed up those Italian cities, how many were asking what father, if he had the power to prevent it, would have allowed such an immense disaster to fall on his children. Men never knew before, as we know now, how hard it must be in our moods of scientific observation to turn our faces toward the mysterious but inexorable power that rules the world and say, "Father."

Yet that is what nearly the whole world is saying in its moods of prayer, so far as it is moved to pray at all. For in these days we have all come to believe that a being of infinite power merely, or of infinite wisdom, but without the moral qualities that would allow us to trust him as a father, ought not to be called God, and would not be worthy of our prayer. Men

of other ages might worship their bloody
Moloch, or Baal, or Mars, or Thor—we
simply could not. So while it is harder
now than ever before to believe in a
Heavenly Father, and pray to him, yet we
must offer our prayer to him, else we shall
not pray. That is the twofold peculiarity
of the present religious situation the whole
world over. And we do pray to him.
Every day more and more of the children
of men are lifting up their voices in prayer
to "our Father which art in heaven."

The historical explanation of this
strange religious phenomenon of our time
is that Jesus, by the compelling power of
his own example, has been teaching the
world to say, "Father." For he himself
said it; spite of all the dark mysteries of the
world, he said it, and he knew it. A volume
of sermons has lately been published under
the title "The Creed of Jesus," meaning by
that title "The Lord's Prayer," and the
title applies with peculiar appropriateness

to the first phrase of the prayer, "Father"; there you have the creed of Jesus himself. Through the whole story of his life, from those early days of his childhood in the temple when he was about his "Father's business," through the scene of his baptism and his temptation, through the whole course of his teaching, in his own prayer in Gethsemane, and his prayer as he hung dying on the cross, always it was "Father."

The one event which has made the deepest mark upon the history of the world is the birth into the world of this one child of our race whose one surest element of faith and knowledge was that the unseen God was his Father. That was truly the creed of Jesus Christ; that is why now nearly the whole world, if it is ever moved to pray at all, finds its lips shaping themselves to say, "Father." Already in all parts of the earth you could find a fulfillment of what Paul wrote long ago in his letter to the Galatians: "Because ye are sons, God hath sent forth the Spirit of his Son into your hearts, crying, Abba, Father." Oh, may the Lord teach us all this lesson. For really I do not believe we can ever master it except as we learn it from him. It must be the spirit of God's dear Son coming into our hearts that should ever enable us to speak so daring a name, and mean it. Some one has well said that "this is a prayer that might be committed to memory in a few minutes; but it is the work of a lifetime to learn it by heart;" and what we want is to learn it by heart, so that we can mean it when we say, "Father."

"Father," yes, but in the prayer it is "Our Father," for there are other children; and we are not to forget these others when we pray. Let me quote you a few sentences from a sermon preached more than fifteen hundred years ago in the old city of Constantinople: "Jesus teaches, moreover, to make our prayer common, in behalf of our brethren also. For he saith not 'My

32

Father,' but 'Our Father,' offering up his supplications for the body in common, nowhere looking to his own, but everywhere to his neighbor's good; and by this he at once takes away hatred, and quells pride, and casts out envy, and brings in the mother of all good things, even charity, and exterminates the inequality of human affairs; and shows how far the equality reaches between the king and the poor man. . . . For to all hath he given one nobility, having vouchsafed to be called the Father of all alike.'' The slow passing centuries have taken nothing from the truth of those words spoken so long ago by St. Chrysostom. Jesus was laying the foundation, not of Christian charity alone, but of a universal democracy, with the whole doctrine of freedom and equal human rights, when he taught us in praying to say, ''Our Father.'' For if God is our Father, it means that we have brothers whom we remember in our prayer.

The attempt has been made sometimes to establish a doctrine of human brotherhood, while forgetting or denying the divine fatherhood. But the success of such attempts has not been encouraging. Take, for instance, that great revolution of 1789 in France. There was a land where the Christian religion had long been discredited by the corruption and greed and heartlessness of its official representatives; and so, when the outburst came, men were impatient to have done with everything belonging to the hated church. Brothers, they would be to one another; but no Father, God; let their worship be rendered to a goddess of reason, or to an opera dancer, or to Robespierre's "Supreme Being"; to anything rather than the Father of our Lord Jesus Christ. Almost everywhere in Paris you can see deeply chiseled in the stone the old revolutionary motto of "Liberty, equality, fraternity"; but those same men were preparing for 1793 and the Reign

of Terror; and again for 1870 and the
Commune. Historically that term brotherhood has now an ominous sound, unless
there be a Father. And so any of us who
really wish to deal fairly with our human
brothers; who really wish to see that
motto of liberty, equality, fraternity,
worked out into a social order that shall
be altogether brotherly, must pratice our
lips and hearts over this prayer which
Christ has taught us to our Father. For it
was Jesus, always knowing himself the Son
of God, who has given us also the one, the
only, effective example of universal human
brotherliness.

I was talking once some years ago to a
poor girl who had not many days to live
and not much breath for speech, and
whispering to me about her own weakness
and weariness of body and of mind, she
said that even when she tried to pray she
could not get beyond, "Our Father." The
saying has often come to me since. If she

had gone as far as that certainly it was a good prayer. And I think the Father could be trusted to fill in for his tired child all that was needed of confession, and thanksgiving, and request. Our Father.

CHAPTER II

Hallowed Be Thy Name

The first petition of the Lord's Prayer. It is to be noticed at the outset that this model prayer begins with requests that have to do with God. In this it resembles the commandments of the ancient Jewish law. For the first table of that law lays down the duties which a man owes to God; only in the second table do we come to the duties that he owes to his fellow-men. When our Lord issued his famous summary or interpretation of the ancient law he followed the same order, for the first and great commandment was of love to God; and the second, which was like unto it, was of love to our neighbor man.

So it is now in the matter of praying. The first three petitions have to do with

God and his glory and his kingdom, and after that we come to the petitions which express our desire for our own good as men.

There are some good people in the world who profess great admiration for Jesus and his teaching and his example, but who quite contradict his teaching and example in this important particular, for what he placed first of all they entirely omit. They profess themselves eager to follow him in his kindness toward men, but they decline to listen when he speaks of reverence toward God. That blunder is to be avoided. If Jesus is worthy of any attention from men it is worth while that we should begin with him where he begins. And with him the beginning of all good things, whether in heaven or on earth, was what he called the glory of God, or the hallowing of God's name. The third commandment of the old law was that a man should not take God's name in vain; now the first petition of the new prayer is that God's name may be hallowed.

There is a wonderful passage in one of F. W. Robertson's sermons in which he argues that "the decay in the meaning of words" is a certain mark of "the decay of national religious feeling"; that "the debasement of a language is a sure mark of the debasement of a nation." And he adds that the name of God may share this fate. "No marvel that we are taught to pray, 'Hallowed be thy name.' We cannot pray a deeper prayer for our country than to say, 'Never may that name in English stand for a lower idea than it stands for now.'" In offering this prayer we ask that we and our fellow-men may be enabled to keep the third commandment, that we may never take God's name in vain, that we may be saved from all flippant irreverence of speech.

One would think that by this time this particular prayer might have been answered, this particular command might have been obeyed. For this sin of profanity is so needless and objectless, so repulsive to all refined taste, so degrading and coarsening to the sinner. Nothing in the world to be gained by it, everything in the world to be lost by it. But the prayer is not yet fully answered, that commandment is not yet fully obeyed; the same old sin goes on, and heaven is still insulted by this harsh and monotonous chorus of profanity rising from every corner of the earth where men have taken God's name in vain. It still sounds like a confession of the sin of our people, perhaps our own, as often as we pray, "Hallowed be thy name."

But you notice the petition in the prayer takes a positive form, while the language of the older commandment was negative. "Thou shalt not," said the law, and a man might have flattered himself that he was secure against breaking the commandment

40

if only he was careful enough never to speak the name of God at all. And perhaps that is as far as some of us have advanced in our practice of reverence in our common conversation; for fear of swearing we have left the name of God severely alone.

But evidently, even if that was obeying the commandment, it would be no true answer to the request in the Lord's Prayer. "Hallowing God's name" cannot mean the same thing as burying it in oblivion. For remember what this latest and dearest name of God is, as Christ has just been teaching it to us, "Father," "our Father." How would any other father feel toward the use of his own name in the language of his children? He would be grieved, certainly, if he ever heard them speaking it in tones of disrespect. And yet if this offense had been committed because the child was angry or thoughtless, blurting out his words under some strong provocation, or

41

letting them slip without perceiving how much they meant, in such a case any sensible father would make allowance and easily forgive or ignore the childish fault. But how must a father feel if his children never spoke to him at all, never spoke of him at all, never once named his name in their familiar speech?

We may well tremble to think how God's ear is still wounded by this harsh chorus of profanity rising from the lips of his enemies in every corner of the earth; but are you sure that the Father's ear may not be still more cruelly wounded by this strange conspiracy of awkward silence which so often falls upon his own children when we ought to be speaking our Father's name?

If we are careful not to grieve the Lord by any profanity of speech, we must be equally careful not to grieve him by our irreverent and ungrateful silence. "Men conscious of deep and real reverence," Robertson says, "are not fearful of the

appearance of irreverénce"; and he goes
on to show how in the days of the great
Hebrew prophets the name of Jehovah
used to be named devoutly and freely; a
mighty cedar would be called a cedar to
Jehovah; a lofty mountain a mountain of
Jehovah; Moses was said to be beautiful
to God. "No beauty—no greatness—no
goodness, was conceivable except as ema-
nating from him." It was in a later and
more degenerate time, when the spirit of
prophecy was dead, that the Jews came to
think the name too holy for human lips;
and even when reading the Scripture in the
synagogue, if they saw those awful char-
acters, always substituted another sound.
They dared not say Jehovah, but offered
the spurious reverence of an awkward silence. It would be well if all who have
learned from Jesus to call God "our
Father" could also learn to hallow his
name by using it more naturally and thank-
fully in our daily speech at home and

among our friends. "Whatsoever ye do," says the apostle, "in word or deed, do all in the name of the Lord Jesus, giving thanks to God and the Father by him."

So much for reverence when we are at home. But what of the reverence that we try to pay to the name of God when we gather to worship him in church? This first petition in the Lord's Prayer may fairly be taken as the divine warrant of the whole institution of public worship. The first desire of all true believers alike being that God's name may be hallowed or honored, we all naturally make it our first business on the first day of the week to come together and unite in showing it honor. "God is a Spirit: and they that worship him must worship him in spirit and in truth," and the Father is seeking such to worship him. It is the will of God that we offer worship. This first petition of the Lord's Prayer is to be associated with all the public services of prayer and of praise. "Hallowed be thy name"—the meaning of every hymn that his people sing, and of every prayer that they offer; of every bended knee or bowed head; of that hush of silence that falls upon those who enter the door of a church—it is all an expression of our common desire that the name of God may be hallowed by us and about us. In everything that we do in our forms of public worship we are endeavoring ourselves to serve as instruments for bringing about an answer to our request that God's name be hallowed.

It is to be noted that this petition stands first of all the petitions in the Lord's Prayer. It is the very first thing that a disciple thinks of as he begins to pray; indicating what must be our first business on the first day of every week—to hallow God's name. Nothing else is to take precedence of that. Other things may follow. Before the day is over it will be right to offer a prayer for daily bread, but that can

45

wait till later. Even the prayer for forgiveness of our sins comes later, and the
prayer for deliverance from temptation
comes later. In Christ's order earliest of
all stands this petition that the name of
God our Father may be hallowed.

It reminds one of the oft-repeated declaration of the psalmist that he will make his
worship of God the very earliest business
of the day. "Awake, psaltery and harp,"
he cries; "I myself will awake early. I will
praise thee, O Lord, among the people." "O
God, thou art my God; early will I seek
thee." "Early," what a favorite word it
is with him! Naturally so for a man who
could go on to say, as the psalmist says,
"My soul thirsteth for thee, my flesh
longeth for thee in a dry and thirsty land,
where no water is; to see thy power
and thy glory, so as I have seen thee in
the sanctuary." A man who felt so
strongly on the subject would not be
apt to be late. "Early will I seek thee."

In another place the psalmist cries to God, "O satisfy us early with thy mercy; that we may rejoice and be glad all our days."

So in the Proverbs we hear Wisdom saying, "Those that seek me early shall find me." So the prophet cries to God,[7] "With my soul have I desired thee in the night; yea, with my spirit within me will I seek thee early." And so in the Gospel story on that memorable first day of the week certain women were early at the sepulcher, and it was they who were able to come back telling of the vision of the angels, and that the Lord was alive. All these devout and highly favored souls seem to have accepted the logic of the Lord's Prayer which puts this request for the hallowing of God's name earliest among all the petitions; not late, but early.

So anyone who had learned the Lord's Prayer by heart would find that this

[7] Isa. 26 : 9.

"early" is a proper word to be associated with all the exercises of the public worship of God; not late, but early. Those who have made an appointment with him, or with each other, that at some specified time we will unite in showing honor to his name, if we are really anxious that his name should be honored, will expect to be at the rendezvous on time. Of course our best endeavors at promptness do not always succeed. The common agencies of transportation cannot always be depended upon to live up to their schedule. Sickness and accident will sometimes disarrange the best of human plans. Once in a while in traveling you even miss your train. We could hardly approve a rule that locked the church door against every late comer, for it might shut out some poor publican who most needed to come in. Indeed you have known some of the very saints of God who because of bodily infirmity had to content themselves with only part of a service; and

48

the part they were hungriest for might sometimes be the Lord's Supper at the end, so they are compelled to come late.

But making allowance for all such occasional accidents and exceptions, it is not putting the matter too strongly to say that where Christian people have agreed to unite at some specified time in showing honor to the name of our God, those who are really anxious that his name should be honored will take pains to be at the place of rendezvous on time. We should be most unwilling to form part of a belated and hurried procession struggling noisily toward their places two or three or five or ten minutes after time, thus confusing the thoughts, and hindering the worship, and perhaps ruffling the spirits of their prompter fellow-Christians who had taken pains enough to be in their places on time. The rule for catching a train is "better ten minutes early than one minute late"; and that is a good rule for church going. "I

myself will awake early." "Early will I
seek thee: my soul thirsteth for thee, ...
in a dry and thirsty land, where no
water is; to see thy power and thy glory,
so as I have seen thee in the sanctuary."
Yes, this is the first of all the petitions
in the Lord's Prayer, and it prescribes
a very resolute promptness in our public
worship.

But this prayer for the hallowing of
God's name ought to be finding an answer
in many other ways and other places be-
sides the public services of the church, or
even our own habits of daily speech. We
ought to have that due sense of all God's
mercies "that our hearts may be un-
feignedly thankful, and that we show
forth his praise, not only with our lips,
but in our lives; by giving up ourselves to his service, and walking before
him in holiness and righteousness all our
days." "Hallowed by thy name," and by
the very ordinance of baptism that sacred

name has already been placed on almost every disciple. Every man or woman who can be called in any sense a Christian is to that extent a namesake of Christ, a namesake of God.

How much it means sometimes to be the namesake of a man; that a child should bear a name that has been greatly honored among men because of the honored father who bore it before him. There is no sadder tragedy in this world than when such a child, by his own unworthiness, drags the honored name that he bears into the mud. It is a strong motive to honorable endeavor, when the child is of any fineness of sentiment, that he has been charged with so sacred a responsibility that it rests with him to honor or to disgrace his father's name.

So Christ has made us aware of a like responsibility as namesakes of our Father God. If a man have any fineness of sentiment at all this must give him a very strong motive for honorable endeavor. "Let your light so shine before men." Why? that they may praise you for your brilliance? No; that is not the reason given; that would be rather a petty and childish motive for a Christian; but "that they may see your good works, and may glorify your Father which is in heaven"; that the name of your great namesake may not be dishonored in you. It is a very searching prayer—a prayer that concerns itself with every single word and deed of our own daily life—when as God's namesakes we pray, "Hallowed be thy name."

It concerns, too, our feeling toward our neighbors; for whether they know it or not, every one of them still bears about upon him, however defaced, something of the divine image and superscription. The stamp on the old coin was Cæsar's, but the stamp on the man is God's. And when we pray that God's name may be hallowed we are laying upon ourselves some grave responsibilities as regards our treatment of that fellow-man.

"Lord, teach us to pray," said the disciples; and our Lord's teaching in the whole subject of prayer was by his own example, and once he set an example for the offering of this first petition that God's name might be hallowed. It was in those last days of his life, when it was growing clearer to him that if the corn of wheat was ever to bring forth much fruit it must fall into the ground and die. In that dreadful apprehension he cried, "Now is my soul troubled; and what shall I say? Father, save me from this hour: but for this cause came I unto this hour. Father, glorify thy name." That was what he should say. That was the petition in which Jesus himself could find rest from all his perplexities; "Father, hallowed be thy name."

CHAPTER III

Thy Kingdom Come

The second petition in the Lord's Prayer has to do with the great subject of our Lord's teaching—the kingdom. At the very outset we read how he "went about all Galilee, . . . preaching the gospel of the kingdom." We read on through the parables and find one after another telling of the kingdom. But what does the term mean? What did Jesus mean when he bade his disciples pray for the coming of this kingdom?

Our Lord's Jewish hearers would have been apt to suppose that they understood the meaning of the prayer, for it was a prayer that they had long been in the habit of offering. And every time they offered it they would be thinking how their own people lay helpless and ashamed under the

heathen power of Rome. To their minds
the coming of God's kingdom would mean
that he would in some way manifest his
divine power to break that hated Roman
yoke and make his people Israel once more
an independent and powerful nation, as they
had been a thousand years before in the
glorious times of David and Solomon,
with some anointed son of David a king on
the throne, so mighty in conquest that all
the other nations of the world must bring
their tribute up to Jerusalem. Something
like that was what every devout Jew had in
mind when he prayed for the coming of the
kingdom. Listening to Jesus, after a while
some of them began to question whether
he, showing, as he did, such strange power
over men's souls, might not be the long-
hoped-for Messiah, God's appointed king
to deliver and rule his people Israel. At
one time many of the common people hoped
that this was so; and even the hostile
rulers could not quite repress their fears

that it might be so; that Jesus himself might be the king who was sent to rule over this long-hoped-for kingdom of God.

This expectation that Jesus might be the king was rudely shaken by his crucifixion, but not permanently destroyed; for it soon revived among his disciples in the form of a belief that he who had been shamefully crucified would speedily come again to reign in power and great glory. In some sense this hope of our Lord's second coming in power is a hope that we are all bidden to cherish. But sometimes the disciples have read into this hope some of the worst errors of the old Jews—that selfish Jewish provincialism, that crude Jewish materialism, which Jesus was always rebuking and correcting. We used to suppose that these more extreme millennarian opinions were characteristic of the more ignorant and fanatical sects. But strangely enough similar views have lately come to be the fashion among certain scholars who con-

sider themselves especially advanced.
They do not shrink from declaring that
our Lord himself based his own gospel on
such Apocalyptic extravagances as you find
in the book of Enoch.

They will hardly persuade us. What
Jesus had in mind when he preached the
kingdom of God was not the triumph of an
oriental dynasty, exalting its favorites and
destroying its rivals. The heart of the
Christian world knows better. The late
Professor Bruce spoke for a sounder
scholarship when he said "that the out-
standing characteristics of the kingdom, as
Jesus conceived it, were spirituality and
universality." Men asked, "When is it coming?" and he answered: "It is now here in
the midst of you"; "It cometh not with observation"; "It is like a seed cast into the
ground, growing, men know not how"; "It
is like the mustard seed, too small to be
noticed, but growing up to the full measure
of a tree"; "It is like heaven hidden in

three measures of meal, and working through the mass till the whole is leavened." What is the kingdom? You ask an apostle, and he answers, "It is righteousness, and peace, and joy in the Holy Ghost." In other words, it is essentially spiritual in its nature, and therefore universal in its operations. And whenever and wherever those divine qualities exist among men there the divine kingdom is already establishing itself; but we are still to pray for its coming, because those divine qualities need always to be made more common everywhere among men than they are anywhere yet. Righteousness and peace and the joy that is in the Holy Ghost are too rare as yet.

Maurice has said somewhere that our Lord, in preaching the kingdom, was "the Revealer and Asserter of the divine order; that he entered into conflict with the anomalies which disturbed that order." "The divine order," meditate on that phrase.

Another has well said that [8] "Jesus employed the phrase kingdom of God, or of heaven to indicate that perfect order of things which he was about to establish in which all those of every nation who should believe in him were to be gathered together," and so forth. And so our Lord himself says in his great Parable of the Judgment, that when the day comes that shall gather all nations before the throne of glory—in other words, when the kingdom is come—the king shall say to those on the right, "Come, because ye fed me when hungry," and so forth; and to those on the left, "Depart, because ye did not." That is, when the kingdom is come visibly and in the largest sense, and when the principle of the kingdom is fully revealed, it will prove to be this simple rule of fairness and kindness and peace; for the king himself when he appears shall

[8] Thayer's Greek-English Lexicon of the New Testament.

speak that out as his own will, and beyond question the will of the king must be always and everywhere the law of the kingdom.

And really, however it be with conflicting schools of interpreters, the larger world outside has not found it impossible to get at Christ's meaning in this phrase. Rather it is a phrase that well-disposed people seem to delight in more and more. Perhaps for the reason that other kings have gone out of fashion we incline more to talk of the kingdom of God. A kingdom means authority; it means an order that must not be violated, laws that cannot be set aside even by the largest majorities; and such laws and such authority we must have.

We have learned to use the same expressive word in other connections. We divide the whole visible universe into kingdoms—the mineral kingdom, and the vegetable, and the animal. No one would think of saying the animal democracy, or the vegetable republic; the principles that rule in those domains are not to be passed upon by any noisy parliament of beasts or of plants; those laws are not to be debated but obeyed. So Jesus has taught us that if we wish well to the world of mankind we must pray for the coming of the kingdom of God among men. And I venture to think that this parliamentary era in which you and I live needs more than any age that preceded it to dwell upon this thought and offer this prayer.

But before speaking further on this point let us turn for a moment to the third petition of the prayer, for the second and the third cannot well be held apart, "Thy will be done in earth, as it is in heaven." "In earth, as in heaven," Jesus says, and that phrase "in heaven" looks back toward the opening address to "our Father which art in heaven." But where is that place heaven? The word means originally the great expanse of the sky over our heads; and when men supposed that the earth was flat and immovable, perhaps as often as they turned their eyes upward they felt sure that they were looking toward the exact locality of heaven. We who know that we rush through a black abyss of space on a whirling ball, would grow dizzy if we should attempt any such precise location of the throne of God. "Upward?" Which way is upward? Is it as we look, or as the antipodes look? As it is always when the talk is of spiritual truth, we are listening to the language of figure when we speak of the sky as the place where our Father is. But the old figure need lose none of its expressiveness because of the newer astronomy. For a man to look upward means as much now in our common thought as it ever meant before Copernicus was born. "To look up, not down," to "seek those things which are above"; you do not need an interpreter to tell you what those words mean. They mean a confession that there are some things above you, and that you will have to climb to reach them. So they mean a confession of your own present inferiority. It is the language of humility and of aspiration when you talk of looking up. The other attitude would be of conscious superiority, to look down; or of rivalry, to look about on a level, comparing ourselves either in a complacent or quarrelsome fashion with those who would be counted our equals. But the moment you begin to look up you have to remember that it is you who are down. Now Christ has taught us to direct our prayers upward, to a Father who is in heaven. Far up in the sky—for no eye can reach to the top of that altitude. To use another fine Hebrew term, he is the Most High God. To look toward the Most High, every other being must turn his eyes upward. The very first phrase of the Lord's Prayer, turning our thoughts upward, puts us into a mood of humility, and of unending aspiration. "Our Father which art in heaven."

But now we return to this third petition that God's will may be "done in earth, as it is in heaven;" and do you not see the magnificent idealism of it, the unlimited discontent of it? For the very wording of the prayer throws us out of any possible complacency with such inferior doing of God's will as has yet been attained anywhere on earth. Heaven, the very top of the sky, is a place where God's will is done properly; and when our Lord imposed on us the habit of thinking of heaven every time we begin to pray, it shows that a perfect doing of God's will, and nothing short of that, is the measure that you and I are to try for, if our prayer is sincere, this very morning.

For, of course, if a man prays honestly for the doing of God's will the first place where he must hope for that doing of God's will is in himself. We pray against any half-hearted compromise by ourselves with disobedience; as if we ourselves were to be

content to do God's will a little and stop
with that; to serve God in one or two mat-
ters, but for the rest serve Mammon. No,
no; for in our prayer we have deliberately
set before ourselves this perfect measure of
obedience, "as it is in heaven," at the
summit of perfection, in the very home of
the Most High; and nothing short of that
will suit us for our own obeying. One of
the old fathers[9] uses the beautiful comparison that "as the sailors pulling at the
anchor rope do not drag the anchor to
them, but drag themselves up to the anchor;
so those who are offering this petition do
not drag God's will down to the level of
their own desire, but drag themselves up to
the holy will of God." And as this Lord's
Prayer is a pattern of all true Christian
praying, so it may show that the end of
all our praying is not that our will should
be done by God, but that God's will should
be done in us. Under the light of that

[9] Clem. Alex. Strom IV, 23.

great truth how many of the mysteries and perplexities of this subject disappear; when we remember that the final end of all true praying is not that our will should be done by God, but that God's will should be done in us. May the Lord himself teach us to pray from our hearts that God's will may be done in us and by us here on earth as it is done in heaven.

We have already recalled our Lord's example as the most effective part of his teaching. If you took this form of words as a form merely it might soon have been forgotten or never learned; but Jesus' own example in prayer was what men could not forget. Because he was always crying, "Abba, Father," therefore we have been remembering to say, "Our Father"; and because he prayed, "Thy will be done," therefore we have been learning, but with slow and stammering utterance, to pray after him, "God's will be done."

You remember how and when Jesus offered that particular prayer. No doubt he was always offering it every day in his own heart; but the place where he spoke it out loud, so that others overheard him and the record has come down to us, was in the Garden of Gethsemane—"Father, if this cup may not pass away from me, except I drink it, thy will be done." There is his own example for that third petition. It may not always be wholesome for us to try to anticipate our graver spiritual crises prematurely. In praying as in other things the better rule may be to take no thought for the morrow. Providence appoints for us bright days with the Beatitudes as well as dark nights in Gethsemane; and while the day lasts let us rejoice in the light of it. But some day or night every man must expect to come to the place where for him to pray honestly for the doing of God's will shall mean to follow the example of Christ in the Garden; and whenever that day comes you may well thank God that you have such an example as his to follow.

So the perfect doing of God's will for which we pray ought to begin in our own hearts; but, of course, it ought not to end there; and that brings us back once more from the third petition to the second, with its broader thought of the kingdom. We are now ready to understand what the kingdom for which we pray must be; a state of affairs, all the world over, among all nations and among all men, when God's will shall be done on earth as it is done in heaven.

For our prayer is that this kingdom should come on earth; we need not pray that it may come in heaven since it is there now. Heaven, wherever it be located, means the place where God's throne stands now, where his rule has never been questioned. But we pray that the kingdom may come also upon earth, in this rebellious and desolated province on the far-off edge of all things. That God's kingdom may come here is what we are to pray for, and with nothing short of that can we as Christians ever be content.

By what means that kingdom of God is to be established on earth we may not clearly know. It might have been established—it is not impossible to conceive of it—as those devout Jews of the earlier time anticipated, by the wisdom and virtue and overwhelming personal influence of some noble human leader, some later and better son of David. It might be so, for one can hardly set limits to the influence that may be exerted by a man, if he be man enough. Or the kingdom might be established—yes, may be, I do not care to contradict it—as the early Christians generally supposed, by the visible return of Jesus in the clouds, thus renewing his personal influence upon the hearts of men. That might be the method. But by whatever means it may be brought about, the essential characteristic of this kingdom is that men's hearts are to be so transformed by the spirit of Jesus that in all their relations to each other God's will shall be done in them and by them here on earth, as it is done in heaven. Without that, no matter what else happens, the kingdom would not come, and with that, no matter what else does not happen, the kingdom would be here. That God's will should be done in men and by men and among men everywhere here on earth as it is in heaven, will be the kingdom of God, and the answer to our prayer.

But what is God's will? Who will tell us that? We offer this petition that God's will may be done, but who shall show us what the will is? For "no man hath seen God at any time," and therefore what man can have any sure knowledge as to what God's will should be like? There it is that we come back once more to our conscious dependence upon Jesus. For we do know him, and the God to whom we are praying is the Being whom Jesus called Father. And we are sure the Son is like the Father, which means that the Father is like the Son; there is no slightest division of sentiment between them: their will is all one. And so this kingdom for which we are taught to pray, the disciples themselves would sometimes speak of as the kingdom of God, and sometimes as the kingdom of Christ—they seem to use the terms indiscriminately, as if it mattered not which phrase they used. The final result—the full meaning—was the same either way, for the will of Christ is the will of God; and what the will of Christ was, and is, we know.

At least we can know if we wish to know it; the means of discovering it are all here. This Gospel is one long declaration of the will of Jesus Christ as to what men ought to be as God's children, and what they ought to do, and how they ought to bear themselves, one toward another, as God's children. The will of Jesus is not hidden from us; and the heart of the world begins to understand that all our own highest dreams of freedom, justice, liberty, equality, fraternity, human blessedness, are included in what Jesus willed for his fellows. So men of all sorts are claiming Jesus as their own representative, the great Reformer, Socialist, Emancipator, Leveler; whatever their favorite title for the attitude of discontent against wrong, they claim Jesus for that. And they do not misjudge him in making such a claim. But what some of them still need to learn from Jesus is that all this freedom and justice and blessedness can be possible only in what he called the kingdom—a kingdom of God. No nation will ever be fit to govern itself freely except as its citizens are severally learning how to obey God. We as freemen are not fit to make laws for each other until we ourselves have some sense of the sacred authority of the law of right-

eousness itself as established by God. Just
as you will not have any true brotherhood
of men except through the fatherhood of
God, so you must not look for any true
democracy of men except through the kingdom of God. Lacking that, you must expect
that your political agitations will give you
license, anarchy, intolerance, violence; and
then again imperialism, the man on horse-
back, the whole dreary circle to be gone
through again; for political science is
rather a dismal branch of study unless you
can attack it in the attitude of faith, and of
prayer for the kingdom of God.

So we do well to speak much of the kingdom. Especially in this democratic age it
is a healthy instinct which has been leading
so many earnest people to magnify the
thought of a kingdom, to lift our hopes
often, above these wretched injustices and
disorders that now curse the world, to the
kingdom; a region somewhere above the
reach of noisy parliaments and congresses,

where laws are not to be debated and voted upon but obeyed. We do well to remember that the "one far-off divine event to which the whole creation moves" is nothing short of a kingdom of God. And day after day, as often as we repeat the Lord's Prayer, our hopes are lifted toward that region of high and holy and triumphant ideal.

"Our Father which art in heaven, Hallowed be thy name. Thy kingdom come. Thy will be done in earth, as it is in heaven."

CHAPTER IV.

Our Daily Bread

The Lord's Prayer has begun with three petitions which are concerned directly with God, the hallowing of his name, the coming of his kingdom, the doing of his will.

But now we are to study the latter part of the prayer which is concerned more directly with ourselves and our own human needs. Here also the petitions are three in number, and the first of these is a prayer for bread. Let no reader fail to observe that this stands first of the three; the other two prayers which have to do more directly with man's spiritual needs come later, but these primary needs of the body are attended to first.

In saying this we do not forget that the whole prayer has begun by lifting our thoughts toward heaven and God. The beginning of all was spiritual and universal. "Seek ye first the kingdom of God, and his righteousness." But now when the time comes that we may properly turn our thought toward those things that are necessary for ourselves, Christ allows us to recognize frankly the physical basis of life, man's daily need of bread for his body's hunger.

This creature whom we call man has been strangely compounded of spirit and body, but in the order of nature the body claims earliest attention. "Not first that which is spiritual," the apostle says, "but that which is natural; and afterward that which is spiritual."

And Jesus allows and encourages us to recognize this same order even in our habits of daily prayer. Some of us might not have expected this teaching from him; for we remember a certain record in an earlier chapter of the Gospel which sounded as if a request for bread could hardly be admitted to the Lord's Prayer at all; or, if admitted, must creep in only as a sort of appendix at the end. I refer to the record of his own temptation in the wilderness, when after long-continued fasting he became aware of his own bitter hunger and felt the impulse to use his miraculous power for changing the stones of the wilderness to bread that he might eat. But Jesus would not do this, answering rather that man shall not live by bread alone. The words might seem to argue a complete indifference to all these bodily needs, whether his own or others. But evidently that would not be a right understanding of what our Lord said. Whatever be the lesson of that temptation scene, it cannot mean that Jesus was indifferent to men's bodily necessities; for here stands this petition first of the three, this cry for bread.

And this order in the prayer is true to Christ's own habitual conduct. The people had noticed a contrast in this respect between him and his great forerunner, John the Baptist; for John came neither eating nor drinking. John inclined to the ascetic ideal; he would forget, so far as possible, that a man ever needed to eat at all. John's scheme of reform was to exalt the spirit by the utmost possible mortification of the flesh. And there was a grandeur in such resolute self-control which the people felt, and to which our Lord himself afterwards bore witness in the strongest terms. But John's path was not the path which Jesus himself chose to walk in. The people themselves felt that he differed from his predecessor; and some of them had commented upon it unfavorably, saying that "the Son of man came eating and drinking." What his enemies proceeded to say about him in this respect was a slanderous falsehood, but it was true that Jesus differed somewhat sharply from John; for Jesus so frankly recognized the needs of the body, and wished that they should be satisfied.

Indeed it is to be noted that Jesus was one whom any host would be glad to invite to his table; for we know that all sorts of hosts did so invite him, one day a publican, and another day a Pharisee. Nor were the friends in Cana afraid that his presence would cast any gloom over the festivities of a wedding feast.

It is quite in character then, when our Lord was offering a model of prayer that should serve for all sorts and conditions of people, that, among all the things that a man might need for himself, he suggests that we ask first for bread.

Can you not feel a more than human wisdom in that order? Does it not help to explain the saneness of Christian morality, as contrasted with that of other men who have felt intensely on religious subjects, a Mohammedan dervish, for example, or a Hindoo Yogi? By Christian I mean, of course,

the morality of the New Testament; not
the more or less imperfect copies of it that
you might find in some convent or other
churchly modification of the New Testament. I mean the standard of morality
which plain men have found rising before
them when they have been content to take
their notions directly from this book. And
I say that as contrasted with the standards
of other men who show anything like the
same spiritual earnestness, the Christian
morality is apt to impress you as peculiarly
sane. And the reason is that it so frankly
recognizes these solid material facts at the
basis of our human life. Christian morality stands upon the earth; it is not "up in
the air," as the saying is. With all its
glorious visions of the new Jerusalem it
does not forget that a living man will need
bread to eat. "Moral ideas rule the world,"
Emerson said somewhere, "but at close
range the senses are imperious"; Chris-
tianity remembers that, and knows how to

deal with life at close range. When a man is hungry its first thought is to have him fed; and it knows that a man must grow hungry unless he has food to eat.

"Our daily bread." Commentators have sometimes enlarged on the modesty of this request. The prayer is only for bread, not for stalled oxen, or for fatted calves, or for any of the other emblems of luxury and excess. And it is a modest request; yet I cannot help thinking that the more significant fact is not the modesty of the request, but that this request should stand here at all.

Our daily bread. That word "daily" has stirred up a good deal of discussion among the commentators—the Greek word, I mean, *epiousion*—for no one has been quite certain what the word means. The word has not been found in other Greek writings, or in the New Testament, except in this one verse in Matthew and the corresponding verse in the Gospel of Luke.

We have to guess its meaning from the context and the derivation.

From its derivation it might possibly mean "our needful bread." You will find that rendering suggested in the margin of the Revised Version; you will also find there as an alternative reading, "our bread for the coming day." Many good scholars incline to this latter rendering, "Give us to-day bread enough to last through to-morrow." If that be what it means, it would show how a man may hope to obey Christ's other command that we "take no anxious thought for to-morrow, saying, what shall we eat," and so forth. For the surest way to avoid all painful anxiety about to-morrow's bread is to carry the subject to the Lord in prayer now.

I do not know which rendering is the more accurate, but practically they all come to much the same thing; our familiar "daily" covers the whole thought well enough. It is a modest request, but a very urgent one; for it stands here first among all the things that we ask for ourselves, and it is a prayer that we expect to repeat every morning as long as we live: "Give us this day our daily bread."

"Give us," for really the bread must be a gift from God. The richest man in the world, or the poorest, has no other source of supply, no other ultimate source. "He causeth the grass to grow for the cattle, and herb for the service of man." Whoever does the sowing or the reaping, yet it is "God that giveth the increase." Prone, as we all are, to a foolish pride and self-sufficiency, we ought to train our lips to this entreaty for bread as a gift from God. The kind Father of all must continue his bounty else we the children will starve. And if we can always remember that the food all comes from him as a gift, perhaps it will make some of us more thoughtful how we take the gift, and what we do with it. If the bread is all a gift from God, why should

I be clutching for more than I can possibly eat, when some other child is left so hungry? Can that be the will of the Giver of the bread?

"Give us this day"—"us." It does not say, "give me." As old Matthew Henry says in his commentary, "This shows that those who eat together are to pray together." Everyone has felt that the wording of the Lord's Prayer fits it wonderfully for the uses of a praying household. For one of the strongest bonds of family unity is this custom of sitting down together to eat. It would be a very poor substitute for a home that should leave it for each to devour his dinner by himself in some solitary corner, like a dog growling over his bone. No, the joy of the day's feast is, of course, that we can come together to eat it; and so the Lord quietly assumes that every household of his disciples will wish to begin the day by coming together to ask for it. "Give us," they say. Some other form of words would have been more natural if he had been issuing a manual for private devotion.

But when you say, "give us," are you going to mean only the three or four or eight or ten who live beneath your own roof, and stop with them? When we started the prayer by saying, "Our Father," did it mean that God was the Father of those three or four or eight or ten who make up your own little family group and of no more? Plainly not; it is to God the Father of all that we pray, and it is to that same God that we say, "Give us our bread." Surely, if we stop to think of it, we must know that that means more than me and my own house. Yes, the request has a modest sound, but really it is a very big prayer nevertheless. In the name of all the children we come to the Father of all and ask for "our bread."

I can fancy two little hungry-looking urchins appearing at my door some sharp morning, speaking this same prayer for bread; and I, pitying their hunger, issue my orders that it be set before them, as much as I suppose that two such small objects could eat. This is done, but still they stand waiting. And when I ask with some impatience what they are waiting for, is not this enough? they tell me that there are a dozen more of them at home. For it appears that these two, rather abler-bodied than the rest, were sent out as messengers in behalf of all of them; and they are afraid that these two portions furnished for them would not go round. So it meant more than I at first supposed when they begged, "Give us bread."

Are there not many times more than a dozen other children in the background every time that you and I come to our Father and say, "We are hungry, give us bread"? If we are faithful to the errand on which we have been sent that will be a very big prayer. But I am afraid we offerers of this prayer have not remembered always how big a prayer it is; we have contracted that generous word "us" too nearly to the dimensions of the smaller "me."

Perhaps the Lord has shown that he understood the prayer more generously than the petitioner understood it. When I said, "Give us," thinking of only my small house, he was thinking of all those other children. And so in answer to my request he in his wise providence gave me bread for myself and for my house, and as much more as I seemed able to carry for all the others also. But what have I done with it all?

If when those two little beggars appeared at my door I had known about the other hungry children at home, and knowing had loaded the two down with enough and to spare for themselves and the dozen others also; and if, going out the door an hour later, I had found the messengers still seated on the steps endeavoring to crowd the whole provision into their own small persons, I should have something to say to the little gluttons; but would that be so very different from the spectacle on which God looks down as regards the distribution that we men have sometimes made of his bountiful answer to our prayer for bread? It should quiet some of us with a deeper sense of responsibility when we think how big a prayer you and I have offered this morning when we, in a world of hungry people, prayed to the Father of all, "Give us our bread."

But now that our thoughts have been enlarged to take in all the other hungry children, will you notice once more that this first request that we are taught to make (for them as well as for ourselves) is for bread? That is to say, under Christ's sane leadership our Christian good will for our fellow-men starts out with a frank recognition of their physical necessities. There will be other things, and greater things, to come after. "Man shall not live by bread only," as Christ said. Other things come later; but when a man is very hungry you can hardly expect to bring in these other things before. At close range the senses are imperious and will not be denied. When our Lord saw the hillside covered with a great multitude of people who had had nothing to eat all day, he was moved with great pity for them. He said that he was unwilling to send them away fasting. He ordered his disciples to go and see how many loaves of bread they had, and then he made the multitudes sit down and he fed them, enough and to spare. All four of the Gospels tell the story; we count it one of the greatest of our Lord's wonderful works; one of the clearest signs to show what his feeling was toward men and how he would wish to deal with them. And you find in that miracle of the loaves this same frank recognition of the physical basis of life that we find in the prayer. It shows that in the order of time the needs of the body will sometimes take precedence of the higher needs of the spirit; that at close range the senses are imperious; that there are conditions when all the other interests of human life will have to await the providing of a loaf of bread.

James, that most practical of apostles, spoke quite in the manner of his Master when he said, "If a brother or sister be naked, and destitute of daily food, and one of you say unto them, Depart in peace, be ye warmed and filled"—in other words, you speak them an edifying sermon—"notwithstanding ye give them not those things which are needful to the body; what doth it profit?" James shows this same sane and practical regard for those things that are needful to the body which Christ has taught us in the order of petitions in his prayer.

We sometimes hear criticisms of the more

practical church activities of our day on the ground that all these philanthropic and humanitarian enterprises are outside the church's proper sphere. I should like to quote an answer to such criticisms which came not long ago from the rector of Grace Church, New York City, a man very highly esteemed for sobriety of judgment. "The institutional church," he writes, "has to bear two reproaches. On the one side are the socialists with their cry that the day has gone by for ecclesiastical methods of doing good, that what is wanted is not charity but justice. . . . On the other hand are those who complain that for the Lady Ecclesia to soil her hands with work of any sort is *infra dignitatem*, and that what is wanted in these religiously dead days is not the institutional but the inspirational church. To the socialists' complaint we answer: 'Go ahead with your scheme for making society perfect by legislation at the hands of imperfect men. If you can work

your Utopia without the preliminary
trouble of converting selfish people into un-
selfish ones, do so.' . . .

"To the inspirationists, on the other
hand, we answer: 'Yes, you are right.
Institutionalism of any and every sort is
but a poor affair unless it has the breath of
God back of it to propel, and within it to
enliven.' But why assume that churches
which try 'to do things' are bereft of that
blessed possession? Why doubt that it is
possible for a city church to be at once inspirational and institutional, alive to the
deep things of the spirit and alive also to
the everyday needs of man?"

Those are wise words and worthy of
careful consideration by all churches and
all Christians. Every church may be, and
ought to be, both alive to the deep things
of the spirit, and also alive to the everyday
needs of man. In all the churches of Christ
his disciples are to go on offering the
prayer which he has taught us, a prayer for

everyday needs; and as often as we offer it we must try to remember the many other hungry children. "Our Father, give us this day our daily bread."

CHAPTER V

Forgive Us Our Debts

We are studying now the latter part of the Lord's Prayer, which has to do more directly with ourselves and our own human necessities. First came our bodily necessities, for the first of these petitions was a prayer for bread. But following hard upon that first petition comes one that springs out of a spiritual necessity for forgiveness. This prayer for forgiveness is closely joined by the conjunction "and" to the previous prayer for bread. "And forgive," "intimating," says Matthew Henry in one of his quaint comments, "that we must pray for daily pardon as duly as we pray for daily bread." What do those complacent individuals purpose to do with this prayer, who have persuaded themselves that they have already arrived at perfect holiness and need no daily pardon?

When we come to this request for pardon for the first time it may seem that our Lord's own example has partly failed us. Among all the prayers that he offered while on earth we have no record of any that included any sort of confession of personal sin. Explain it how you will, that is the one most striking phenomenon connected with the life story of Jesus Christ; that he whose presence was always throwing other men—and even down to our own day continues to throw other men—into a mood of personal confession of unworthiness, never once offered any such confession for himself. "Which of you convinceth me of sin?" he cried to his adversaries, and no one has yet taken up the challenge successfully.

No, when Christ would offer us a concrete example to show how we must do our praying for pardon, he does not bid us look

95

at himself, the Master, but at a certain publican who had gone into the temple one day to pray; and who durst not lift up his eyes unto heaven, but smote upon his breast, and said, "God be merciful to me a sinner." "To me a sinner." The parable teaches that in praying for forgiveness one need not be very much afraid of egotism; the first person singular has a good right to stand in that prayer, and the publican used it there. The Pharisee did not; he preferred to keep his confessions of sin in the third person. Other men are the sinners, extortioners, unjust, adulterers, "this publican"; the Pharisee was fluent at confessing the sins of these other men, and he thanked God that he himself was not like them. And probably such pharisaic confessions in the third person have been offered even in our day.

A little prayer meeting was organized a good many years ago, at a time of spiritual interest, by some small boys living on Mur-

ray Hill, New York; and on one occasion
two of these boys had drawn into their
meeting a youthful neighbor whom they did
not regard as being in a hopeful state of
grace, thinking that the meeting might do
him good. There were only the three of
them present that day, the two small saints
and this small sinner. The present report
of the meeting comes from one of the two
saints, who is now a doctor of divinity,
highly honored throughout the church. He
reports that the service began properly
enough with prayers of confession from the
two saints; but each of them took it upon
him to confess the other's sins, not his own;
and they did this with such unmistakable
and pointed frankness that the moment the
second "amen" had been spoken the two
jumped from their knees and flew at each
other's faces in a fistic encounter which had
to be checked by the kindly intervention of
the small sinner whom they had brought in
to be converted. The children are instruct-

ive because of their transparency. The human virtues and the human foibles show through. And here were two little Pharisees of the nineteenth century who had not yet learned the great publican lesson that confession, like charity, begins at home. We must try to learn that lesson, and never to let the truth slip out of our memory, when we are confessing sins, that we are to begin with our own; that we are to do our confessing not as Pharisees, but as Christians. "God be merciful to me a sinner."

And yet in the prayer it says, "our debts," not my debts. For in all these petitions of the Lord's Prayer, God's children are expected to be praying together, sharing, so far as we can, each other's burdens. There are such things as common burdens of debt, or of ill desert; and a man of Christian temper will not be too careful to excuse himself from his own fair share in them. If the whole family be found at fault in any way, or the whole church or the whole community, it is fair to assume that some part of the blame rests on me, a member of the group; and that I will need some of the forgiving. The Pharisee tried to forget that; he would make haste to say, "I am not as bad as the rest of them, thank God;" but the Christian would say rather, "Forgive us; I am one of them."

That was a deep cry of penitence which came from the prophet Isaiah when he saw the vision of the Most Holy God, and cried, "Woe is me! for . . . I am a man of unclean lips, and I dwell in the midst of a people of unclean lips." The prophet felt that his own soul was smirched by the black stain of his people's impurity.

Was there ever a more truly Christian confession of public guilt than that which was offered by that great President of the United States who in his second inaugural spoke of the offense of slavery, and how

God was giving "to both North and South this terrible war as the woe due to those by whom the offense came"? Mr. Lincoln's own sentiment is more clearly revealed in a letter which he wrote to a friend a few days later, in which he said that this was a truth which he thought needed to be told, "and, as whatever of humiliation there is in it falls most directly on myself," he says, "I thought others might afford for me to tell it." It is the language of a Christian, not a Pharisee; a man who knows how to put his confessions of sin into the first person.

Yes, and even our Master himself, though he had no sin of his own to confess, came very near to accepting a share of the responsibility for the sins of the rest of us. And the people felt this, all the people felt it. Even the guiltiest of them, when they looked upon Jesus, were apt to gain some sense of the completeness of his sympathy with them. One of them spoke of him long afterwards as a Being who was "holy,

harmless, undefiled, separate from sinners'';
but another also said of him that he "bare
our sins in his own body on the tree."
Even though Jesus was undefiled and could
never ask forgiveness for any sin of his
own, yet it has been a most precious element of the Christian faith that his prayer
has been going up with ours as often as we
make common cause in our need of pardon,
and pray God to forgive us our debts.

It is to be noted that the word in this
petition is ''debts.'' In Luke's shorter
version of the prayer the word is ''sins'';
but here in Matthew's fuller report it is
''debts.'' And do we not find ''debts'' the
larger, more searching word? For it will
include the meaning of the other word.
Every sin becomes of necessity also a debt;
for the sin was a withholding of some
obedience that we owed to the divine command, and leaves us hopelessly insolvent to
God unless it can be forgiven. But some
things that we had not thought of as posi-

tive sins are debts. When a man, talking of his own faults, calls them sins, you might take that to refer only to the positively wicked things that this man had done; but when he calls his faults debts, you cannot help thinking also of the many good things that he had failed to do.

If some day I snatch a man's purse, everybody knows that to be a sin; but suppose I had only failed to pay that man the money that I owe him, what is that? At least everybody must know that that leaves me in debt to him. So if some day I push a man into the water and he is drowned, that is a sin, the sin of murder; but suppose he has fallen into the water, and I, seeing it, would not take the trouble to help him out, what is that? If some day I deny my Lord's name or blasphemously dishonor it, that is a sin. But suppose he is looking for some friend to confess his name and I hold my peace, what is that? Evidently I owe him something that I have not paid. This idea of debts and the paying of them is a broader idea than that of merely not committing overt acts of sin. There are sins of omission, and the language of the prayer reminds us that they are real sins, too, and that they need God's forgiveness quite as much as the sins of positive commission.

Indeed in Christ's Judgment Parable, which sheds so much light on the meaning of his prayer, these sins of omission are the only sins referred to. The wicked who stand on the left hand of the Judge are not charged with any positive wrongdoing. No doubt some of them had done their share of evil deeds, but these are not referred to in the trial. The good things that they had not done make up all the counts in that indictment. "I was an hungered, and ye gave me no meat: I was thirsty, and ye gave me no drink: . . . Inasmuch as ye did it not." They had left undone the things that they ought to have done, that was the gravest charge against them; that was what made them such miserable sinners. That was the great debt which needed to be forgiven.

The daily repetition of this word debts ought to make our consciences more sensitive to that side of our daily obligation which includes the things that we ought to do, so that if we fail to do them there is our sin. We are so apt to develop a false complacency because we have not been doing much harm, not so much harm as many other men; we have never killed anybody, we have never broken in to steal, we have never committed perjury against a neighbor. These accusations of positive and criminal wrongdoing do not ruffle our serenity. "Let the galled jade wince, our withers are unwrung." But have we done anything at all? That is the question. Or how much have we done of all that our Master put us here to do? The great burden of the world's guilt is not made up of its sins of commission; not at all; those

are bad enough, but at the worst they are
occasional and often accidental. But it is
these lifelong, uninterrupted sins of omission that have been heaping up that intolerable burden which only the infinite goodness of God can ever forgive. "Inasmuch
as ye did it not"; and that is the kind of
sin that presses most heavily upon our
hearts when we come up to our Father
praying, "Forgive us our debts."

But we are not to drop off the rest of
the petition, "as we forgive our debtors."
For we have no reason to expect that God
will forgive us unless we are forgiving, too.

The question has often been asked how
sin ever can be forgiven. And some, perhaps, would answer that it never can be.
Every offense drags its penalty after it by
an unfailing sequence. Retribution is an
impregnable fact; every debt will have to
be paid somehow; but evidently this prayer
breathes a better hope; we as Christians
hope that sins may be forgiven by our

Father, but how and why? and what grounds can we have for any confident assurance about it?

All who have ever sat at the table of the Lord would be apt to answer that our hope of forgiveness is in "the blood of the new covenant which is shed for the remission of sins." It is because Christ once "suffered for sins, the just for the unjust, that he might bring us to God." Guilty souls have been finding peace because they have felt that in some way Christ, by what he did and suffered, has won forgiveness for us, and is able to offer it to us. All Christians may well be glad to remember those grounds of our confidence as often as we repeat the Lord's Prayer. It is because Christ our Saviour has taught the prayer to us that we can repeat so confidently this petition for a forgiveness of our debts. The prayer properly brings large beliefs and hopes and assurances to us for the reason that it came from the lips of him who afterwards gave his life for us on the cross.

Nevertheless the wording of the prayer itself does not introduce any such reasons for hoping for God's pardon. At the time when our Lord was teaching his disciples this prayer they did not yet know how he must die on the cross. But here in the plain wording of the prayer he does give them another reason for hope in God's forgiveness, and one that they could already understand; "As we forgive our debtors," he bids them say. If we men can forgive our fellow-men that is good reason for believing that God will be able to forgive us. If I already know of forgiveness as an actual fact in this world, a principle now operative as between me and my debtors, then all those theories of invariable retribution will have to adjust themselves to this known fact; if I can forgive, why should not God? It is a most comforting thought. As Calvin says, "The Lord intended partly to comfort the weakness of our faith; for he has added this as a sign, that we may be as certainly assured of remission of sins being granted us by him as we are certain and conscious of granting it to others." And Matthew Henry says that "If there be in us this gracious disposition it is wrought of God," and so "encourageth a hope that God will forgive us."

Yes, but suppose there is no such gracious disposition in us; suppose that even when we are approaching God in prayer for forgiveness we are refusing to forgive. Why, then the prayer itself becomes an imprecation; we are beseeching God by our prayer not to forgive us our sins, since we forgive not. And as Calvin says, "What do such persons gain by their prayers but a heavier judgment?"

Evidently our Lord was very much in earnest about this particular phrase, for it is the only one that he takes up again and explains further after the prayer was ended. "For if ye forgive men their trespasses," he says, "your heavenly Father will forgive you: but if ye forgive not men their trespasses, neither will your heavenly Father forgive your trespasses." At a later time he took up the same thought yet once more and gave it still further treatment in the Parable of the Unmerciful Servant. That servant who had been forgiven by his master the hopeless debt of ten thousand talents went out and found a fellow-servant who owed him a hundred pence, and took him by the throat, and would not listen to his cry for mercy, but cast him into prison until he should pay the debt. And the lord was wroth, and revoked his pardon, and delivered this unmerciful servant to the tormentors till he should pay all that was due.

The parable shows that there are two worlds in which men live; a world of rigid retribution where every debt will be exacted to the last farthing, and another world of mercy, forbearance, forgiveness; and we men can have our choice which world we shall live in, but we cannot live in both. We cannot be taking forgiveness from God and at the same time refusing forgiveness to men. And so, as St. Chrysostom says, "We ourselves have control over the judgment that is to be passed upon us." If we can forgive and do, so will God.

Yes, "if we can forgive"—oh, but how hard and impossible a condition that sometimes becomes. How can you forgive? You find this petition for forgiveness resolving itself into one that God will enable you to do some forgiving. Well, when you get as far as the attempting of that task then you find yourself walking once more safely in the steps of our great Example. Jesus might not ask forgiveness for himself, but where was another like him for forgiving others? It was when men were nailing him to the cross that he prayed, "Father, forgive them, for they know not what they do." We do well to seek the help of that Example when we pray, "As we forgive our debtors, so forgive us."

I have quoted already from the greatest of American state papers, that second inaugural, where the ruler of a nation was making confession of the nation's sin; but you remember that before the paper ends it contains another and equally Christian proclamation of forgiveness: "With malice toward none, with charity for all"—the world quickly learned those wonderful phrases by heart—"to bind up the nation's wounds . . . to do all which may achieve and cherish a just and lasting peace." Lincoln's last legacy to his people was this message of mutual forgiveness. It is a message which we all wish to accept and appropriate. As we ourselves hope for the forgiveness of God, we must learn to do our share of forgiving. This is to be a daily prayer with us. It springs from a need as constant as the need of daily bread.

"And forgive us our debts, as we forgive our debtors." "For if ye forgive men their trespasses, your heavenly Father will also forgive you: but if ye forgive not men their trespasses, neither will your Father forgive your trespasses."

CHAPTER VI

Temptation

As the Lord's Prayer draws toward its close it brings us under a deep sense of spiritual need. For the past the need is of forgiveness, and so the prayer has asked for that. As regards the future the need is of deliverance, and so the prayer goes on to ask for that.

"Lead us not into temptation." Many readers have been perplexed by this request, and perplexed for one or the other of two quite different reasons. On the one hand some say, "How can we suppose that the good God ever would lead anyone into temptation, and therefore why ask him not to?" So we read in the Epistle of James, "Let no man say when he is tempted, I am tempted of God: for God cannot be tempted with evil, neither tempteth he any man."

If God tempteth not any man why should we offer a prayer that seems to imply that except for the prayer, God might tempt us? It is evident that this difficulty was felt almost from the beginning, for more than one of the early fathers [10] quote another reading as sometimes given in their day, "Suffer us not to be led into temptation." But it takes little reflection to show that this difficulty goes deeper than any particular wording of the prayer; for it grows out of the fact, everywhere observed but so impossible for us to explain, that moral evil has somehow gained entrance to a world under the power of a holy God; a fact which we can never hope to explain, but which everywhere forces itself on our attention. Of certain things, however, we can be sure; and one is that God himself would never tempt a man to sin. For tempting is not the same as leading into a

[10] Cyprian De Dom. Orat. 25; Aug. De Serm. Dom. IX. 30.

place where one might be tempted. The latter, God might do and often does. The Gospel history relates how Jesus was "led up of the spirit into the wilderness to be tempted of the devil." The tempting was not God's doing, but the leading was. A human father would not tempt his son, but he might send him to college in spite of the well-known fact that some new temptations will assail him there that he never met at home. The tempting is in no way the father's act, but the sending is. "Give me neither poverty nor riches," says the wise man in the Proverbs, "lest I be full, and deny thee . . . or lest I be poor, and steal." The good man recognized peculiar temptations coming from excessive wealth on the one side and from excessive want on the other; and he is wise enough to pray that he himself may never be led into either of those perilous extremes. But in the providence of God some men have been poor and other men have been rich. It is not then a meaningless or superfluous request when we say, "Lead us not into temptation."

But sometimes men have felt another difficulty in offering this petition. Since it is a well-known fact that the highest development of spiritual character comes so often through resisting temptation, how could it be right for us to pray that all temptation be abolished? James himself, the very apostle who teaches us that God never tempteth any man, had already declared in the same chapter, "Blessed is the man that endureth temptation: for when he is tried, he shall receive the crown of life." And Peter cries, "Beloved, think it not strange concerning the fiery trial"—or temptation —"that is to try you, . . . but rejoice"; and elsewhere tells his readers that the trial of their faith is "much more precious than of gold that perisheth, though it be tried with fire." So Jesus himself speaks his richest promises to those disciples who have continued with him in his temptations. Altogether the Scripture makes it very evident, as indeed we ourselves know from our own observing, that this perilous experience of temptation sometimes offers men the highest kind of spiritual opportunity. It serves as the refining fire for purifying the gold. Shall we not be condemning ourselves to perpetual spiritual immaturity, or else to hopeless spiritual mediocrity, if we beg God not to lead us into temptation? "Blessed is the man that endureth temptation."

> Temptation sharp? Thank God a second time!
> Why comes temptation but for man to meet
> And master and make crouch beneath his feet,
> And so be pedestaled in triumph? Pray,
> Lead us into no such temptations, Lord!
> Yea, but, O thou whose servants are the bold,
> Lead such temptations by the head and hair,
> Reluctant dragons, up to who dares fight,
> That so he may do battle and have praise![11]

And our souls thrill in response to this martial aspiration of Browning's good

[11] Browning, The Ring and the Book.

pope, and we are almost on the point of praying that temptation may come, that so by doing battle against it we may have praise, or by faithfully enduring it we may have the promised blessedness.

But no; that is not the prayer that Christ has left for us to learn and offer. Rather let it be our daily request that God shall lead us not into temptation. Blessed is the man who endures it when it comes, but we are not to pray for it. "Lead us not."

For any man who was himself asking for the temptation or—what is much the same thing—himself willfully running into temptation, is a kind of braggart; and instead of being strengthened by the experience is more likely to be overthrown by it. It is as if he were saying boastfully: "Try me against this famous tempter of yours, and see how easily I can put him to flight. You tell me of others whom he has tripped up and destroyed, but they are not so bold or so strong on their feet as I am. Try me and see."

In the early days of persecution there came to be a kind of frenzy among some of the Christians; they would go and deliver themselves up to the authorities and insist upon the honor of martyrdom, as if to say, "Put me to the test, and see how boldly I shall pass through the fiery ordeal." The wiser leaders of the church were compelled to check this recklessness by threatening heavy spiritual penalties. Real martyrdom was the highest blessedness; but to seek it in this way made a man a suicide, not a martyr.

In the gentler conditions of life appointed for us in these later days a man may show the same vainglorious spirit in some other way. He may pray God to send the temptation of sorrow and loss upon him, that he may show how patiently he can bear it. Or being of a different temper he may insist on forcing his own way into companies and associations that have proved morally disastrous to many of his neighbors. When you remonstrate with him, he replies easily: "No fears for me; I am not a baby to need to be tied always to some one's apron string. I can look out for myself. If temptations come I need a little exercise at resisting."

Our Master would not encourage in us any such spirit of vainglory, but rather a mood of humility, a sense of personal danger, a prayer for deliverance from these awful incitements to sin. "Watch and pray, that ye enter not into temptation: the spirit is willing, but the flesh is weak." And when our Lord offered that counsel he himself had been praying, "Let this cup pass from me"; for that cup had brought him the cruelest temptation ever suffered on earth;—"Let this cup pass from me." Though he added also, "Not my will, but thine, be done."

If you turn back to the earlier scene of

our Lord's threefold temptation in the wilderness you find that the first assault was when, being hungry, he was tempted to make the stones bread; but this he would not do, showing how hunger or any other trial, when it comes in the way of God's providence, is not to be refused; rather a child of God may gain blessedness and strength by bravely enduring it.

The second temptation was quite different from the first. In this Jesus was tempted to throw himself down from the pinnacle of the temple, which he refused to do; showing how the danger of falling or any other trial, when it does not come in the way of God's providence—when the man himself had rashly and needlessly pushed himself into it—will not strengthen his soul, and will not bring such promise of blessedness. No; for a man to push himself into any such peril or temptation is not trusting God or serving him, but tempting him, and "Thou shalt not tempt the Lord thy God."

So the principle is that when these temptations come, as they often will, we are to
face them patiently and fearlessly; but all
the while our own personal desire and
prayer to God must be, "Lead us not into
them." To put it into everyday language,
when God sees fit to bring us into any of
these trials we shall do our best with his
help to bear them manfully; but if it were
left for us to choose we prefer to stay out
of them. For we have not found in ourselves any moral strength to spare. So,
conscious of weakness, our own preference
would be, "Lead us not into temptation";
and that is the proper prayer. "Let others
confide as they please," says Calvin, "in
the native abilities and powers of free will,
which they suppose themselves to possess;
it is enough for us to stand and be strong
in the power of God alone." Yes, Christ
taught us a prayer of wise humility and
also of trustful courage, "Lead us not into
temptation, but deliver us from evil."

And it is to be remembered that a man in offering this petition does not pray for himself alone. All through the Lord's Prayer we have been made conscious of our fellowship with other worshipers. We are speaking to our Father; we pray for our daily bread; we ask for the forgiveness of our debts; and so here "Lead us not into temptation." We are to be thinking of all these other tempted souls as well as our own soul—and of all other souls that ever might be tempted—when we say, "Lead us not."

Evidently no man could offer any of these petitions honestly unless he himself was doing his best to bring about an answer. When we pray, "Give us this day our daily bread," it means that we are deeply concerned for all the other hungry members of the family, and are willing to do what we can toward getting them all fed. Simply to pray for them without the doing, simply to say, " 'Depart in peace, be ye warmed and filled'; notwithstanding ye give them not those things which are needful to the body; what doth it profit?" says the practical James. So when we pray for forgiveness for our debts we are thinking of all the other indebted members of the family who may need forgiveness as well as we, and in our prayer we announce in so many words our determination to do our part toward furnishing such forgiveness as they need. "Forgive as we forgive," for we are going to do our part of the forgiving.

So when we come to this awful peril of temptation, our prayer is that we may not be led into it. "We," it means all of us; for we are thinking of ourselves and also of these other imperiled souls about us, and praying for them all while we pray for ourselves. And, of course, that must mean a willingness and strong determination on our part to do whatever we ourselves can toward keeping them all out of temptation and delivering them all from evil. What

an absurdity it would be—not to say blas-
phemy—for a man to speak this prayer to
God and then rise from his knees and go out
of the church door and willfully place in
some brother's way some stumbling-block or
occasion to fall. No, no; "it must needs
be that offences come; but woe to that man
by whom the offence cometh!"

Temptation then is a fact in this world,
a fact always to be taken into our calcula-
tions. It would be a delusion (and a perilous delusion) for any of us to suppose that
the world is soon going to be so recon-
structed that a man will be able to take his
journey through it, and march into the
heavenly gates, without the trouble of meeting and overcoming temptation. No, that
will never be. It must needs be that of-
fenses come; but our own part as humble
and compassionate children of God is to try
to bring about as nearly as we can, for ourselves and neighbors, that condition where
men shall no longer be tempted to sin. So

far as we have any power for arranging things, we are to make it, according to Gladstone's maxim, "As easy as possible for men to do right, and as hard as possible for men to do wrong"; we are to take stumbling-blocks out of the way of unsteady feet, and to place all the safeguards we can about those tempted souls who are likely to fall.

In one sense we may never hope to succeed in this attempt; for whatever we do the path heavenward will always remain hard climbing; the broad and easy road along which a man can travel without effort will still be the road downward that leads away from life. Temptation and difficulty and peril will still do their salutary work in this world; "it must needs be that offences come; but woe to that man by whom the offence cometh!" "It were better for him that a millstone were hanged about his neck, and that he were drowned in the depth of the sea," than that he—through his own

greed, or malice, or selfish indifference—
should cause some little one to stumble.
This closing petition of the Lord's Prayer
leaves us face to face with this dark and
perplexing fact of moral evil and spiritual
peril—a fact that no one can afford to
treat slightingly, a fact that must often
send a child of God to his knees in a kind
of agony of prayer.

For this prayer would bring us to feel
that the saving of men's souls and charac-
ters is the one thing most to be desired;
and the ruin of men's souls the one thing
most to be dreaded; and a thing very much
to be dreaded because the forces within
the man and round about him, working for
his ruin, are so terribly strong. "For we
wrestle not against flesh and blood," Paul
cried, "but against principalities, against
powers, against the rulers of the darkness
of this world, against spiritual wickedness
in high places." He speaks under a sense
of impending danger, of perilous conflict.

And with this same sense of peril Christ has brought us to our knees with what sounds almost like a cry of pain and terror, "Lead us not into temptation, but deliver us from evil"; or, if you will, you may read that last phrase, "Deliver us from the evil one."

And so the prayer abruptly ends, as if it were intended that we rise from our knees with those two solemn sayings of Christ still ringing in our ears, "Watch ye and pray, lest ye enter into temptation," and, "Whoso shall offend one of these little ones, . . . it were better for him that a millstone were hanged about his neck, and that he were drowned in the depth of the sea." "Deliver us from the evil one."

There remains to consider a very beautiful expression with which we have been taught to close the Lord's Prayer, "For thine is the kingdom, and the power, and the glory, for ever. Amen." In Luke's report of the prayer these words do not occur, and if you turn to the Revised Version you find that they are absent from Matthew's report also. The oldest manuscripts do not contain them in either Gospel, but indicate that the prayer, as Christ taught it, ended with the words, "Deliver us from evil."

This additional sentence seems to have been at first the response made by the congregation when the prayer ended. A little later it was written into some of the copies of the Gospel itself. They form a beautiful and fitting response, and as such we do well to continue to use them, for they help us to remember, or else show that we have not forgotten, those large requests with which the whole prayer began; that God's name should be hallowed, that his kingdom should come, that his will should be done, on earth as in heaven. It was so that Christ taught us to pray first of all. And now at the end we are glad to return from the sense of our own human weakness and peril, and from the whole dark mystery of temptation and spiritual ruin; lifting our thoughts once more to God and his perfect goodness, and the certain triumph of his cause. The end of true prayer is always a confident hope in God. "Look up," cried the Lord to his disciples, "and lift up your heads; for your redemption draweth nigh."

> What though thou rulest not,
>   Yet heaven and earth and hell
> Proclaim, God sitteth on the throne
>   And ruleth all things well.

"Alleluia: for the Lord God omnipotent reigneth." "For thine is the kingdom, and the power, and the glory, for ever. Amen."

CONCLUSION

In His Name

We have been studying the petitions of the Lord's Prayer; a brief prayer, but, brief as it is, we have found that it holds a world of meaning. One thing, however, the prayer does not hold, one word that has grown specially dear and familiar to us in our Christian worship, and that is the name of our Lord himself. A prayer without that name seems to us hardly Christian. Turn to the manual of worship that has been most widely accepted by English-speaking Christians—the Book of Common Prayer—and look at the order appointed for the morning, and you will see that all the other prayers in it, with a single exception, close with some such phrase as "Through Jesus Christ, our Lord," or "This we

131

beg for Jesus Christ's sake," the natural
conclusion for Christian prayer.

> Through him the first fond prayers are said,
> Our lips of childhood frame;
> The last low whispers of our dead
> Are burdened with his name.

But in the prayer which Jesus himself has
taught us that name does not occur. It
may seem a strange omission, but a later
saying of Christ himself furnishes explanation of it. "Hitherto," he said, and this
was at the end of his life, the evening before he suffered, "ye have asked nothing in
my name." And why should they ask in
his name while he was still there with them,
still by his own presence controlling and
indorsing their requests of the Father? It
was after he had been taken away from
them that these men would long to know
that their requests still went up with that
same indorsement as if he were with them,
that they still carried the power of his
name; and so he here gives them this authority.

But even in those earlier days while the Lord Jesus was with his disciples, they had been learning in other ways, if not in their prayer, that his name had great power. To receive even a little child "in his name" had large promise of reward. It was in the power of that "name" that they undertook all their strange works of healing. They came back one day saying to him, "Lord, even the devils are subject unto us through thy name." Indeed the fact of this mysterious power residing in the "name" became so evident that even some who were not true disciples at all would try to avail themselves of it; some to whom Christ would have to say at the last, "I never knew you"; but they would be saying to him, "Have we not prophesied in thy name? and in thy name have cast out devils? and in thy name done many wonderful works?" They had used his name. Even while Jesus was yet with his disciples they were coming to feel that it gave new significance to any word that they might speak, or any deed that they might perform, to say that it was "in his name."

So it is not to be wondered at that after their Lord was taken from their sight these same men still cherished the phrase which already meant so much to them, and that they still made frequent trial of its power, confiding in it more and more as they found how much this name of Jesus would do for them.

We may recall that first great scene of apostolic activity after the Day of Pentecost, the event which first brought the new church to the attention of the rulers as a formidable power which would have to be reckoned with; it was the healing of the impotent man by the Beautiful Gate of the temple. Afterwards when Peter was called to answer for this act before the rulers, he said, "Be it known unto you that by the name of Jesus Christ of Nazareth doth this man stand here before you whole." And that was just what Peter had said to the lame man himself when he took him by the hand, "In the name of Jesus Christ of Nazareth, rise up and walk." Already they had found a power in this name which assured their own confidence as disciples, and which also aroused the apprehension of their adversaries; for the express command which the rulers laid upon these men was that they should not teach "in this name."

So as one reads on through The Acts and the Epistles the evidence appears on almost every page how the name of Jesus Christ was coming to be magnified among those men. They rejoiced when they were "counted worthy to suffer shame for his name"; they were happy if they were "reproached for the name." Their assemblies were gathered "in his name"; they spoke of it as the "name which is above every name"; the name at which "every knee should bow"; the one "name under heaven given among men, whereby we must be saved.'' So every one of them that named that name of Christ was to ''depart from iniquity''; in that name they were baptized; in that name they were justified. Their brightest hope for the world to come was that they should then see his face and ''his name shall be in their foreheads.'' In short, as Paul sums it all up in his letter to the Colossians, ''Whatsoever ye do in word or deed, do all in the name of the Lord Jesus.'

Now if the name of Christ played so large a part in all the thought and speech and action of these disciples, you do not wonder that it also claimed a very large place in their prayer. If they had learned to find some strange power in that name, even when they were dealing with their fellow-men, surely they would not cease to trust in it when they came to deal with God. And so it was in that comprehensive passage which I have just quoted from the

Colossians, Paul ends the sentence by saying, "Do all in the name of the Lord Jesus,
giving thanks to God and the Father by
him." And in similar terms he writes to
the Ephesians, "Giving thanks always for
all things unto God and the Father in the
name of our Lord Jesus Christ." I quote
these familiar passages—a very few of the
many that might be quoted—to show how,
after our Lord's death, his disciples had
grown into the habit of carrying his name
with them wherever they went, and attach-
ing it to all the interests of their lives; to
their words of confession, their works of
help and healing, their patient suffering of
wrong—all was in the name of the Lord
Jesus.

But especially to their prayers; for what
Jesus on the night before his passion told
them they had not done heretofore, hereafter they would be always doing, always
asking good things of the Father in his
name. Indeed the Lord's Prayer itself,

though it does not speak the name of Jesus, would now carry in their own thought—as it still does for us all—the sense of his presence. It was he who taught it to them. It was by reason of his encouragement that they were bold to call God their Father; it was by reason of his indorsement that the guiltiest of them could come boldly asking forgiveness for their sins. So in all their praying—from that day to this—it has been characteristic of all prayer which would be known as Christian that it has been offered in the name of Jesus Christ. So this thing that Jesus told the disciples they had not done up to the time when he left them, since that time they have never ceased doing, asking all sorts of good things from the Father in his name.

But now it is time to raise the question what it means to say that a man is doing deeds, or speaking words, or offering prayers in the name of Jesus Christ. Certainly it ought to mean something more than a

mere repeating of this form of words.
Those evil-doers whom Christ said he did
not know could claim that they had used
that form of words, and repeated it over
and over again: "In his name prophesy-
ing, and in his name casting out devils, and
in his name doing many wonderful works";
but that brought them no nearer to him.
A form of words that is nothing more than
a form, a magical incantation, has no place
in Christian worship; and the more sacred
the words the worse it would be to use them
as a form, and nothing more.

Well then, back of the outward form,
what does it mean when we offer our
prayers to God in the name of Jesus? What
has it meant from the beginning?

For one thing it has meant, in the faith of
Christians generally, a new confidence that
God will answer the prayer. Many a
simple-minded believer could express his
own meaning in some such way as this, "I
myself am not worthy that God should

listen to me for my own sake; but when I
speak in the name of his dear Son, who
loved me and gave himself for me, then I
am sure that God will listen.' So the
phrase, "In the name of Jesus," would
mean nearly what we mean by that other
common phrase, "For Jesus' sake." It
means a new confidence that God will hear
the prayer. Surely we have a right to such
confidence. Surely Christ himself implied
as much when in teaching his disciples this
new form for their petitions he added,
"Ask, and ye shall receive, that your joy
may be full." He intended to give a new
confidence.

Only we must never suppose that God
our heavenly Father needed any such per-
suasion to interest him in us; we must not
think so unworthily of God. Good old
Matthew Henry urges this caution in his
comment on this text: "When we are
taught in prayer," he says, "to plead
Christ's merit and intercession, it is not

as if all the kindness were in Christ only,
and in God nothing but wrath and fury.
No, . . . the Father's love and good will
appointed Christ to be the mediator. . . .
So let it confirm in us good thoughts of
God."

And while I am quoting from that
worthy commentator, listen to one other
word: "'Hitherto have ye asked nothing
in my name.' Nothing, comparatively,
nothing to what ye might have asked. . . .
See what a generous benefactor our Lord
Jesus is; he gives liberally, and is so far
from upbraiding us with the frequency and
largeness of his gifts that he rather up-
braids us with the seldomness and strait-
ness of our requests. You have asked nothing in comparison of what you want, and
what I have to give." Yes, that is true,
too; the words mean that, and so every
time we offer any prayer in Christ's name,
and thereby are made to think once more of
the great reach of his good will toward us

and toward our neighbors, it ought always to affect us with a deeper sense of the pitiful smallness of our own desires. It is as if once more we could hear him saying, as he said to the Twelve: "Is that all? You have asked nothing yet—nothing to what I stand ready to give. Go on with your asking, ask more." Certainly as often as we pray in Christ's name it ought to encourage us to the asking for larger things from God. The new phrase means that.

But more than this, when we speak in Christ's name (whether to God or to men), it means that we, if we are Christians, stand here now as the visible representatives of his earthly mission. The interests that he lived and died for on earth he has now, humanly speaking, left in our charge. We have been constituted a sort of executors to the estate. And in discharging this sacred trust we necessarily speak and act for him. As well as we know how we ought to be always carrying out his purpose, thus doing whatever we do in his name.

Of course to our own thought the relation is not quite that of an executor to a dead man's estate, for we know that our Lord is not dead; though our eyes cannot presently see him, he is still alive to us. But he is not present to the senses of men; and in his apparent absence we have to act for him by some power of attorney, as it were. In this deep and vital sense we must be doing whatever we do in his name; doing for him and in his apparent absence what we believe he would do for himself if he were visibly here.

This should be true of all our work as Christians, and anyone can see how it applies also to our prayer as Christians. When, by the authority vested in us, we pray in his name—that is, when we sign his name to our request—it is in the assurance that this is what he himself would be asking for if he were here. Otherwise we should be violating the trust imposed in us. If, knowingly, you sign Christ's name to some document that he if present would have refused to sign, you are guilty of a kind of spiritual forgery, and that must never be. If ever you feel compelled to ask God for things that you think Christ would not have been willing to ask for, then as an honest man offer that prayer in your own name, not in his.

So this new formula of Christian prayer, while it encourages us to ask for larger things, and with stronger confidence, also imposes upon us a new sense of responsibility; we must deal with him honestly in the use of his name.

"Hitherto have ye asked nothing in my name; ask, and ye shall receive." One can feel a tone of pleading urgency in these words of Christ spoken to these dearest friends of his. For this was his last interview with them before his passion. He spoke as a man will speak to those whom he loves best, and when he is looking into their faces for the last time. I mean for the last time in this present earthly life; of course, we may still hope for later meetings on the other side; but have you ever found that hope of a future reunion to diminish much the pathos of your last meeting with some friend here and now? It was under this deep emotion, looking as for the last time into these faces that had grown dear to him, that Jesus said some things to them that he had never said before. For one thing he told them that as often as they gathered about the table in friendly company to eat together after he was gone, they must be sure to remember him. And that is a request which still moves the heart of every lover of Jesus Christ. The church universal still reads those words into the most solemn act of her worship; we still carve the words in the most sacred part of our house of prayer, "This do in remembrance of me." And it is a request that no friend of Jesus would like to disregard.

But then again at this same last interview Jesus made known to these same friends of his his desire that hereafter they should do their praying to God in his name. Apparently our Lord was earnestly desirous that his friends should treat his name as if it still carried great weight with God and with men.

One can understand that feeling. Some friend of yours is going to some distant country where he is a stranger, but you yourself have been well known; and you give him letters of introduction to those in that country whose acquaintance would be of most value to him. "They will do the right thing for anyone who comes in my name," you say. It would grieve you a little if your friend should decline to use the letters, seeming to disdain your introduction, as if he had not thought your name worth using. So here almost the last word

Jesus spoke to his friends was this generous message of introduction and indorsement. "Wherever you go," he said, "and whatever you need, you can use my name."

These men did not disdain the offer of introduction, but from that time forward they considered that name of Jesus their one most precious asset. You can find the proofs of the value they put upon it all through the later books of the New Testament. We have quoted a very few of the passages which indicate how these early disciples, both in their words to God and in their dealings with men, were eager to do all things in the name of the Lord Jesus. The question occurs whether we ourselves have always shown the same eagerness, whether our Lord has ever been grieved at any of us because, after he had made us this same offer of his name we have slighted the offer. "Use my name," he said, "tell everyone that you come from me." But we shook our heads and set our lips. If so the fault ought not to be re-peated. "Hitherto have ye asked nothing in my name: ask, and ye shall receive, that your joy may be full."

This parting message may well stand at the close of our study of our Lord's in-structions on the subject of prayer. "Lord, teach us to pray," said the disciple; and we have been following his answer to that request. We have found it in that personal example which he was always setting them by his own praying; we have traced it also through the successive sentences of that sacred form of words which he has left to guide us in our supplications. But the in-struction is not completed till we reach this parting message from the Master to his dis-ciples: "Hitherto have ye asked nothing in my name: ask, and ye shall receive, that your joy may be full."

Date Loaned

MAY 8 1958	5/27		
JAN 11 1960			
	tme		
MAY 1 8 1989			

CPSIA information can be obtained
at www.ICGtesting.com
Printed in the USA
BVHW020725100323
659975BV00003B/252

9 781286 061770